The Art of the Deal

An Entrepreneur's Guide to Negotiation, Money Management, and How to Succeed in Business

Table Of Contents

Introduction

Thank you and congratulations for purchasing The Art of the Deal: An Entrepreneur's Guide to Negotiation, Money Management, and How to Succeed in Business. This book will show you exactly how to become a successful entrepreneur, using groundbreaking methods to successfully run a profitable business.

Today it seems to be much more popular than ever to call yourself an entrepreneur. The Forbes 400 list of the richest people in the United States is replete with individuals who have created massive amounts of wealth in only a few short years. Popular TV shows, such as Shark Tank and The Profit, showcase the entrepreneurial pursuit of the American Dream.

At the same time, many people who call themselves entrepreneurs are not business savvy. Furthermore, they possess negative beliefs about money and wealth. Some have difficulties with time management and goal development.

In this book you will find practical directions, straightforward strategies and blunt ideas that will help you to become more successful in the business arena. Upon the conclusion of this book, you will move forward more efficiently and confidently.

The approach taken in these pages is very direct, and it may scare you off. If it does, this is your first lesson: Entrepreneurial life is not a place for those who are easily worried.

On the other hand, fearlessness and determination win the race in the long run and these ideas will help you avoid problems and issues in your business ventures.

Good luck and bon voyage!

Chapter 1 – Get Your Thinking Straight

Starting with early childhood, we are often compared to others and throughout our lives we judge ourselves based upon these types of comparisons. Many times, it starts in the family, when parents measure their children's worth as to who is smarter, who is taller, or who gets better grades.

In school, we are often graded based upon a curve. Unfortunately, this means that only a certain percentage of students can get an A. If someone else receives an A, it decreases the chances for others of getting the same grade.

Comparisons and one-upmanship in popular culture are never-ending. Multiple magazines have lists of "10 most popular X," "30 under 30," or "The most successful Y."

All this leads to the belief that, in order for someone to win, someone else needs to lose.

At an early age we are also introduced to negative connotations about making money. Most of these ideas come from nannies, teachers, or vocational educators. None of these professions are known for big salaries, yet these people teach us about money while we are still developing a belief system.

Let's take a look at some common expressions you have likely heard when growing up:

"hard-earned dollars"

"A day late, and a dollar short."

"poor but honest"

"I never win anything."

"excessive profits"

"those less fortunate"

Motivational coach Tony Robbins conducts a great exercise in which he first he asks his audience what they would do if they were to suddenly get a huge sum of money; say, 10 million dollars. Here are some of the answers that he usually hears:

"I would donate some money to charity."

"I would buy a house for my parents."

"I would help my friends who are in need."

"I would buy nice things for myself."

All of these responses sound quite innocent, don't they? Next, Robbins asks the same students what they have been told about "money" when they were growing up. Here are some of the answers he receives:

"Rich people are evil."

"To make a lot of money, one needs to be dishonest."

"It is impossible to make a lot of money quickly."

Finally, Robbins says, "Do you see the problem we have here?"

Money doesn't care about morality. If it did, there would be no rich drug dealers.

There are plenty of people making money in dishonest ways. At the same time there are just as many individuals doing a lot of good while making money: Elon Musk, Richard Branson, Bill Gates, to name a few.

In order to be successful in business, you need to throw all your negative beliefs about money away. One of the best ways to do so is to read the biographies of successful people.

Two classic books are a must read for any successful entrepreneur: Napoleon Hill's "Think and Grow Rich" and "Psycho-Cybernetics" by Maxwell Maltz.

Napoleon Hill was an American author who was tasked by Andrew Carnegie to interview the 500 most successful people on the planet and find commonalities between them. At the time, Carnegie himself was one of the richest and most powerful individuals in the world.

Hill spent years studying businessmen and inventors such as Henry Ford, Alexander Bell, Thomas Edison. "Think and Grow Rich" is the result of this enterprise.

"Think and Grow Rich" was first published during the Great Depression. By the time of Hill's death in 1970, the book had sold more than 20 million copies.

In 2007, BusinessWeek magazine ranked "Think and Grow Rich" as the #6 best-selling paperback business book of all time. Over 70 million copies had been sold worldwide by 2011 and, virtually, without any marketing.

There is a reason the book is so successful. It gives practical, hands-on advice about the methods that successful business people and entrepreneurs practice. Hill introduces 13 principles that were shared by these influential thinkers of the modern era.

Maxwell Maltz, the author of "Psycho-Cybernetics," was a plastic surgery pioneer.

He obtained his medical degree from Columbia University in 1923. While practicing plastic surgery, he noticed something interesting: people were coming to him and complaining that their looks were a source of the problems in their lives. As a plastic surgeon, Maltz would fix their appearance but, in the majority of cases, their problems did not go away. He became convinced that many of the patients needed more than a surgery and some of them didn't need a surgery at all. This led Maltz to become interested in human psychology. He then wrote "Psycho-Cybernetics," a book about how people view themselves, their negative beliefs, and their thoughts on success.

In his book, Maltz introduces the notion of self-image and the internal dialogue concerning our vision of ourselves. Self-image comes into play when we are thinking about what we can and cannot accomplish; what is difficult and what is easy for us; and the regulation of our relationships with others.

As Maltz accumulated more experience, he became absolutely convinced that what we want in life is primarily restricted by self-imposed, artificial limits.

Maltz was not alone in studying this field of psychology. One of the first pioneers of research regarding self-esteem psychology was Prescott Lesky.

Lesky viewed human personality as a system of ideas, all of which must be consistent with each other. Ideas that are consistent with the entire system are accepted and can be acted on. Ideas that are inconsistent are rejected and the person will undertake no action.

His experiments showed that whether a person would do something or not often had very little to do with the individual's physical or mental capabilities. Their beliefs told them what they could or could not accomplish.

Lesky was a schoolteacher and opportunistically tested his ideas on his students. He decided to see whether a student's difficulty learning certain subjects was due to a student's negative thoughts about learning the subject. He believed that if a student could change his or her beliefs about a subject, the learning ability could change also.

This turned out to be the case. One student, who misspelled 55 words out of a 100, received an average of 91 the next year and became one of the best spellers in school. Additionally, a student who was told by a testing company that he had no aptitude for English won an honorable mention that next year also.

Lesky's research showed that challenges in learning had nothing to do with mental abilities; but, instead, with how students saw themselves and their negative or positive associations with the subject matter.

For example, when failing a test, some would say, "I'm a failure," (which is a broad generalization about oneself) and not, "I failed that test" (which is a true statement about a single event).

Do you have contradicting beliefs about business and money, which are stopping you from succeeding? Find and read "Think and Grow Rich" and "Psycho-Cybernetics." I guarantee that it will be time well spent.

Chapter 2 - Always Look For The Win-Wins

In the previous chapter we established that money needs to be separated from morality. Making a lot of money does not make you a bad person. In fact, the more money you make, the more you enrich the lives around you.

Let's take a look at Bill Gates. Currently, he is worth about 80 billion dollars. It is impossible for a person to make this money by himself.

First, Gates invented and created a product. After demand for his product skyrocketed, he hired programmers, technicians to service the computers, rent office spaces and much more.

Simply put, Gates created jobs and started paying salaries to a lot of people. In turn, these new employees bought homes, cars, enjoyed vacations and continued to spend their money on luxury goods.

Gates also employed a sales force that created marketing materials, bought advertising and continued to stretch the dollar out into the community.

Bill Gates did win in business and because of his win, many people won around him.

This concept just doesn't stop there. Gates lives in a large mansion that overlooks Lake Washington. The mansion is 66,000-square-foot in size. It is known for its design and technology inside. It took seven years and $63.2 million to build. That's a huge contract for a big construction company; not to mention, the jobs created for maintenance personnel and security.

This is the mentality you want to have in business: How can you win and help others win? To take it one more step, when entering new business ventures or negotiations, what can you do so that everybody involved wins?

The win-win mentality is key to a successful business strategy and is very different from "All rich people are evil," or "For me to win someone needs to lose."

Once you find ways to help people win, it will create a lasting symbiotic relationship wherein your business partners, clients, and employees continue doing business with you.

At the same time, it is impossible to build a sustainable business that is based on its customers not getting what they would perceive as a good deal.

Sure, it is possible to build a Ponzi scheme or a short-lived con. However, such a business cannot exist in the long run. Unhappy customers will not be repeat customers, if they don't give you a bad Yelp review first. Furthermore, acquiring new customers is complicated, time-consuming and expensive.

This is not what extremely successful people do. They are not con artists looking for someone to lose while they win because it is not a long-lasting business relationship.

Donald Trump is another great example of a winner.

The secret to his success is simple, yet often overlooked: Donald Trump chooses deals where there is more than one way to win and it is impossible to lose. He wins by default when choosing the right deals.

Let's take a look at few examples of how this works.

About ten years ago Trump picked a fight with the City of Palm Beach in Florida. Residents flying flags on their property are restricted to flagpoles that are no higher than 42 feet and flags that are a maximum of four feet by six feet.

In October of 2006, without getting any permits or discussing it with city authorities, Trump erected an 80-foot flagpole on the front lawn of his Mar-a-Lago Estate and flew a car dealership-sized American flag of 15 feet by 25 feet.

The town council took the bait, citing the oversized pole and flag as violations of the town code. They fined Trump $250 a day for every day the flag and pole remained on the estate.

"The town council of Palm Beach should be ashamed of itself," Trump responded.

"They're fining me for putting up the American flag. This is probably a first in United States history." He went on Nancy Grace's national TV show to complain that the City of Palm Beach was unpatriotic.

Trump then filed a lawsuit against Palm Beach, asking for $25 million in damages to what he called an abridgment of his constitutional right to free speech.

How can Trump lose in this scenario? Sure, he could lose in court, but the publicity he got from the incident would have more than paid for any possible court fees. Plus, he's a patriotic American!

Here is another similar scenario that Trump orchestrated. When Obama was running for President, Trump was one of the vocal "birthers," doubting the legitimacy of Barack Obama's presidency based on assumptions that Obama was not a natural-born US citizen.

Here, again, there was no way for Trump to lose.

If Obama were to have a problem, Trump could have said: "I told you so. I was right."

When Obama showed his birth certificate, Trump said: "I am glad that he sorted this problem out. I was the reason why he has done so."

No matter how things develop, it's a win for Trump. Trump has done it again and again.

The subjects he chooses are so inherently interesting and controversial that they inevitably get incredible amounts of attention and free publicity. Critics of Trump do not understand that by talking about him they are not weakening him. They are only making him stronger.

There are win-wins all around you, too. You just need to learn to spot them.

Chapter 3 – Develop Goals, Vision And Clarity

Virtually every book on entrepreneurship talks about the importance of having goals, vision and clarity.

Many books don't mention, though, that clarity and vision are a choice. They are not a gift or a talent. It's not that some people have them and others don't.

Clarity is something you decide you want and then you work at obtaining it. It doesn't just show up one day by itself.

Every day that you spend on your entrepreneurial journey without a sense of clarity, without understanding what the big goal is or what you are trying to accomplish, is a day that you will probably step in the wrong direction.

You are not going to magically just move towards achieving your vision. You need to have a vision and then you must lay out the tracks to achieve it.

Without conscious and directed action your business won't progress. It will stagnate and drift along. The key is understanding where you need to go and what you need to do. It starts with being honest about where you currently are and where you have been, so that you can make the best possible decisions in your specific situation.

Most people have just an inkling of where they want to go. They have only a slight idea of the present but are masters of knowing the past.

The problem is that the past is the least important and yet that is what they know.

When developing your goals, begin with a long-term view of your life and your business. Practice idealization in everything you do. Create a fantasy for yourself and begin contemplating what your life would look like if it were perfect in every respect.

The biggest single obstacle entrepreneurs have in their business life is self-limiting beliefs.

By underestimating yourself, you set either no goals or goals that are far below what you truly can accomplish.

This combination of idealization and future orientation allows you to cancel or neutralize the process of self-doubt and self-limitation. When you imagine an abstract ideal, you have no limitations at all. You also make no compromises, whatsoever, when it comes to your dreams and desires.

Instead, you project your dreams into the future as if you were one of the most powerful humans on the planet.

Imagine that your work life is perfect three years from now and answer these questions:

1. How does it look?

2. What are you doing?

3. Where are you doing it?

4. Who are you working with?

5. What kinds of skills and abilities do you have?

6. What kinds of goals are you accomplishing?

7. What status do you have in your field?

Chapter 4 - Prepare Better Than Anybody Else

When entering a negotiation or making a deal, many people just jump in to see what happens. This is not the way to approach a business deal.

Your aim is for people to respond in your best interests. This is possible, but it does require a lot of work on your part.

Everybody wants something. Your goal is to find out what it is. Start with doing a lot of research. Find all the information you can about the other party involved in a deal.

Does this person have a LinkedIn page? Facebook page? Twitter? Did they ever write blog articles, maybe even a book? All these things will allow you to build a rapport with the other side.

Next, take an objective look at what is going on and ask yourself, "If I were the other party, what potential problems might I experience or pay attention to?"

For example, suppose you are selling a house that has a really old refrigerator, which is making the buyers unhappy. You could buy a new refrigerator or you could simply say, "I will buy you a new refrigerator if this one breaks within a year." Instead of spending money on a new refrigerator or giving a discount, you are simply giving a one-year warranty that isn't costing you anything at the moment.

The more successful a person you are negotiating a deal with, the less successful is the offer of extra money. However, this does not mean that they cannot be influenced in other ways.

Today, people have very small attention spans. They spend large amounts of time surfing channels on TV or on their phone. Most people are compelled to answer a text message, email or phone call immediately.

Unfortunately, this obsession with electronics leads to people paying very little attention to others. The art of listening is an unused skill.

This is why people desperately search for anyone who can make them feel important by listening to what they have to say. Our culture's lack of hearing what others say provides a gigantic opportunity to incorporate active listening into your entrepreneurial best practices and negotiations. Talk less, listen more.

By learning the art of listening, you will be able to influence people, gain their trust, build relationships and, most importantly, make great deals.

During negotiations, continuously think in terms of leverage. Following are a few examples of leverage that are often overlooked:

1.   Your customers are assets. If you have customers that you have built a relationship with, that trust you and buy from you on a regular basis, then letting others have access to these customers can be an offer of a valuable asset.

2.   A second asset is your brand: logo, menu, order forms, websites, and brand recognition.

3.   Technology and software can also be an asset; whether it is proprietary or applied in a way that is unique. Teleseminars or infomercials are not unique, but using those as tools to build a system for selling can be an asset. These assets can be sold to other businesses or can be exchanged for something that is of value to you.

4.   Another example of an asset that can be leveraged is process. For example, Tupperware is a process-based business.

The value of the company is not in pots and pans that they are selling. Anybody can manufacture pots and pans in China for pennies. The real value and the real asset are contained in the process and system of selling. If you have a system that is working consistently and delivering results, that is an asset you can use in your negotiations.

5.   Reputation is another example of an asset than can be leveraged. Donald Trump and Gene Simmons use their reputation very successfully to license products. Richard Branson is able to start new companies in new niches because of his reputation. Joan Rivers, among other products, was successful in selling cupcakes. She never baked or cooked in her life. However, people liked Joan Rivers and trusted her opinion so they bought her cupcakes.

Always consider the worst-case scenario when making deals and leveraging your assets.

Kevin O'Leary, an investor on the TV show Shark Tank, often asks the participants about what will happen if a bus hits them. This is a really great question to think about and consider. What will happen if something happens to your partners? What is the worst-case scenario when going into a deal? Are you going to lose time? Are you going to lose money? Will your reputation be at stake?

In addition to considering and thinking about worst-case scenarios, be certain to put everything in writing. Even if you trust the person with whom you are about to close a deal, memorialize it on paper.

Here's why: It is only a matter of time when one of you remembers things differently. You may be great friends, you may be agreeing on everything, but there will come a time when disagreement on the details will arise.

Consequently, when this day comes, it is always beneficial to have a piece of paper with everything written down, so that you and your partner can continue to have a positive working relationship.

Finally, if you are getting into business with someone for the first time, a golden rule is to ask for three business references. It is best that you are able to contact three people who have negotiated a deal with this person and would enter a business arrangement with this person again, without reservations. You would be surprised as to how many people cannot come up with three references.

If a potential partner cannot show you three people that are happy after doing business with him or her, what makes you think that you are going to be the first one?

Chapter 5 – Don't Be Like The Majority

Earl Nightingale, a famous motivational speaker, once said if you want to accomplish something, but have no road map, no shortcut, and no teachers, you just need to look at what everybody else is doing and do the opposite. Be uncommon.

If you do what everybody else is doing, you will get the results that everybody else is getting. Results of the majority are average by definition. If you want to be successful, if you want to make more money than everybody else, then do things in a different way.

For example, according to data from the Small Business Administration, 80% of all businesses fail within the first five years of their existence.

Most people are convinced that all that is required to run a business is common sense, yet 80% of businesses fail. This alone is proof that a successful business is a rarity.

Furthermore, the ones that succeed, the going concerns, become nothing but a glorified job, stagnant in outlook. Now you've really cut away almost every single business that is started.

As an entrepreneur, you need to remember this. Do not deceive yourself. Some people have the luxury of thinking that they do all the work in the office and if they weren't there, the business would shut down. Actually, everyone is expendable.

These people are living in a fantasyland and this outlook will not work as an entrepreneur. Put your feet firmly on the ground and live in the world of reality. It is important to see things the way they really are and always be honest with yourself.

Now, let's look at the positive side. Even though the majority of businesses fail, there are also successful ventures that, not only make a lot of money for their founders, but also make a difference in the world.

Here are some great questions you can ask yourself:
What does Larry Ellison know about business that you don't?
What does Bill Gates know about business that you don't?

If you know the story of Bill Gates, you know that he sold a piece of software to IBM before he even developed the software. After he sold the software, he had to find it and buy it! Would you have the guts to sell something that you didn't even have, that you weren't even sure that you could find and acquire before you locked up a contract?

Sam Walton, Richard Branson, Steve Jobs, Donald Trump and Warren Buffet all thought outside the box. They did things differently than the norm, which is why they became billionaires.

They all do not have common sense. They have uncommon sense. They are not usual people and they have built unusual businesses. The reason why all of these people became successful is because they made the right decisions about the right things at the right time. It was not luck and it certainly was not some random event.

Ultimately, a business is a reflection of the founder's skills as an entrepreneur.

Dunn and Bradstreet, the number one credit-reporting agency for businesses, released a study about why businesses fail. They found that 90% do so because of a lack of skills and knowledge on the part of the owner.

This is why I would like to commend you for reading this book right now. You are doing so because you realize that building a business and becoming a successful entrepreneur takes learning skills that you may not possess today.

Now let's take a look at some practical examples of how you may apply uncommon sense and business success principles, like Bill Gates and Warren Buffet did, in your current position.

Assume that you are a sales person in a car dealership. Your first objective should be to identify what every sales person is doing. What do all the sales people typically do? They gather around the water cooler and they wait for customers to show up.

Now that you have identified what everybody is doing, you must endeavor to do the opposite; which means not hanging by the water cooler expecting customers to materialize on their own.

The question is what should you be doing? As a salesman your focus is now implementing strategies to gain customers and sell cars, nothing less.

For example, you can launch a referral program; wherein, every customer that buys a car from you will receive a letter in which you ask them to recommend you to their friends. In this case, instead of standing by the cooler and doing nothing, you are instead at your desk, writing and sending letters to your existing customers and implementing follow up calls.

One of the best car sales people in the country took pictures of his customers with their new cars. He would then put the pictures in his cubicle. He had a large repeat and referral business and, after awhile, he attached newer pictures of the same customers and families next to each other. Upon entering his cubicle, one would see a progression of pictures: a montage of the same people as they were buying new cars through the years. A simple idea, yet very powerful.

No matter what field you are in, there are people in that occupation who are more successful than others. They are successful because they are doing things in a different way.

Most accomplished individuals reach a point in their lives when they have enough money and that is when they start thinking about giving back and sharing their wisdom. Oftentimes, they write books, give speeches and interviews.

Thanks to the Internet, finding information today about successful businessmen and women is easier than ever before, and free.

Find out who are the most successful people in your industry, read their books and interviews, and study what it is that they are doing distinctly different.

It is really this simple.

Chapter 6 - Be Known For Something

Like it or not, we live in a celebrity-obsessed and celebrity-driven culture.

Donald Trump's participation in the presidential elections proves this very well. The first Republican debate of the previous election cycle, in 2011, drew approximately 2 million viewers; the first debate of the current election cycle boasted 24 million viewers. Everything was the same, except for one participant: Donald Trump.

The media continuously satisfies America's obsession with celebrities, be it Trump, Kim Kardashian or the next new star. Unceasing article feeds are released every minute about celebrities: twitter selfie feuds, marriage updates, favorite foods, exercise regimens, children and charitable causes.

Not to be outdone, Forbes Magazine publishes an annual list of the most influential and wealthiest celebrities, which sells as well as the issue about the wealthiest business leaders.

No matter what business you are in, it is influenced by people who are celebrities.

This is why it is really smart to turn yourself into a celebrity, to be known for something.

Now, you do not have to be an Oprah degree of famous or grace the cover of People Magazine. You can be a celebrity in your business niche or in your local area. The smaller the size of your industry or locale, the easier it is to turn yourself into a celebrity.

Arnold Schwarzenegger first earned a sizable fortune as a bodybuilding celebrity. He then used his newfound fame to become a movie star, a businessman and, finally, a politician.

On the local level or in a small business it is relatively easy to become a celebrity: you simply need to insert yourself into advertising spots.

Car dealers and local real estate agents practice this on a regular basis. A doctor in New York City, Dr. Jonathan Zizmor, became famous by plastering his face in New York City subway cars.

No matter the enterprise, self-promotion creates celebrities. Associating with celebrities is beneficial also: any photos posing with a celebrity are valuable within the context of making yourself known.

Grab opportunities to attend receptions with celebrities. Post these photos on your websites, in your newsletters, on Facebook and Twitter. Create press releases regarding your meeting.

There are several reasons for turning yourself into a celebrity in your business.

First of all, you become more interesting to your customers, your prospects and the media. Your status as a celebrity gives your customers bragging rights. It gives them a reason to talk about you. Who wouldn't want to talk about the doctor he or she has seen on TV, has heard on the radio or mentioned in a newspaper? Who wouldn't want to talk about a restaurant owner who just won an award at an international cooking competition?

Turning yourself into both a celebrity and an expert is optimal. Direct Response copywriter John Francis Tighe often repeats the old adage, "In the land of the blind, the one-eyed man is king."

To become an expert you do not need a PhD, an MBA or years spent in school. An expert is someone who knows more than we do. This really is all there is to it.

Therefore, it is often possible to become an expert by simply reading a number of books and educating yourself on the subject in which you wish to become an expert.

Obviously, everybody prefers working with an expert. Who would you rather see for a medical condition? A doctor around the corner that can see you the next day and who has an empty office; or, the top rated specialist in your town, who wrote a book on the subject, regularly appears on the radio and TV, and who has his own blog regarding articles about his or her area of expertise?

Chapter 7 - Follow Up

Most people never start anything. As Woody Allen once said, showing up is 50% of success. Furthermore, those who actually do show up or start a business venture usually don't follow it through to completion.

Many entrepreneurs create value by delivering a product or service to the customers that they truly need, but they never develop sustainable relationships.

A typical business person thinks in terms of transactions. A guest comes to a restaurant, eats, pays and exits. This is a transaction, an event.

Successful people do not think in terms of events; rather, they think in terms of processes and opportunities.

Consider Tupperware, a successful company that sells pots and pans. To a novice it might seem that the value of the company is in the products the company is selling. This is as far from reality as it gets.

Anyone can order pots and pans from China, or from any other seller of the same commodity.

In fact, the real value of the company is the Tupperware process of selling its brand: the Tupperware parties, the follow up and relationships with customers and distributors.

Buying a product or service requires the following criteria:

1.   Prospective buyer must have a need or want

2.   Prospective buyer possesses the money to be able to pay for a product or   service

3.   There must exist a reason to act right now

The fact that your deal is not finalized today does not mean that it will not go through tomorrow, or the day after tomorrow.

Let's consider a few examples from daily life. Upon using a business for the first time, like a restaurant or a dry cleaner, how many times do you receive a follow-up letter inviting you to come back?

Have you ever received a refrigerator magnet as a gift so that you will have their business phone number handy at all times? How many businesses send you an interesting newsletter each month? How many businesses are investing time and effort into building a relationship with you? The answer, most likely, is hardly any.

The problem here, again, is that businesses see you spending money as the main event. The sale is where it begins and ends for them. Smart business people understand that the process before and after the sale creates the lasting relationship with the customer; individual aspects surrounding the sale like saying "thank you," asking for referrals or inviting them to come back.

Success, money, wealth and standing out all go together. The rarer the piece of art, the dining experience, or the first edition of the book, the higher the price.

Many times it is hard to find what makes you stick out in a crowd, especially if your business is a commodity. However, what you can do in each and every situation is deliver value, relentlessly and diligently follow up, and build relationships. This can be applied in any business.

It is relatively easy to sell a product or a service to a group who is already interested in the product; yet, most people have difficulties prospecting or finding people that would be interested in their product or service in the first place.

Usually businesses utilize cold calling to find customers; in essence, trying to sell their products and services to those who are probably not interested. More often than not, this turns into a futile exercise.

As mentioned earlier, more and more people are experiencing low attention spans. According to Yankelovich Consumer Research Agency, in the mid-70's we were exposed to approximately 500 advertisements as opposed to as many as 5000 ads today.

Ads permeate everyday life: on news websites, watching TV programs, riding the subway, or driving past billboards on the highways.

This is why so many people today have ADD and ADHD.

We live in digital times. Our inner biological rhythms are rushed. Our days are broken up into bits and bytes. We skim across instead of going in deep. We race without pausing to consider where we are really going. We have wired up outside, but are melting down on the inside.

We take pride in the ability to multi-task and walk around with iPhones, iPads and fitness trackers and are surrounded by instant reminders. Everything is designed to help us cope with our numerous responsibilities.

People enjoy describing themselves as "24/7," taking pride in a life where work and being active are intermingled and never end.

This lack of attention and constant bombardment of stimuli makes it nearly impossible to sell to a person learning about a product for the first time through a cold call approach.

Successful selling in today's world uses target prospecting, coupled with follow up.

You don't want to blindly sell to anybody; instead, first identify potential buyers that are likely to be interested in your product or service.

Trying to sell a yacht to someone who lives in the middle of a desert is not a good idea. The prospect should have a logical reason to be interested.

Determine a link between your offer and why someone would want to buy from you. For example, if you are selling furniture, then target homeowners. If selling expensive, exclusive furniture, then target homeowners in certain zip codes.

The next step is to create an environment or selling point where the homeowners who might be interested in your furniture raise their hands and express an interest in buying new furniture.

You want to make it easy for people to raise a hand and tell you that they are interested. In order for this to happen apply incentives: a free guide or a free video, for instance. People who request a guide or a video will leave you their contact information and you then follow up knowing that you are dealing with interested prospects and someone who is predisposed to buy.

Chapter 8 - Protect Your Time

Time is your most valuable asset: time to think, time to create a business, time to network, time to solve problems, time to build sales funnels and time to create marketing.

It is important to define your peak productivity. Unfortunately, many people ignore this aspect of planning when defining objectives. Today, people work faster and harder than before, clueless as to whether they are actually getting anywhere.

Before you can be productive, you need to specify your goals. Then create a plan that will bring you measurably closer to your goals. Once you have a plan and quantitative benchmarks in place, begin measuring your productivity and managing your time.

A worthwhile exercise concerning time management is calculating the value of your time.

First, determine how many hours you are currently working. Next, divide the amount of money you earn by your hours worked. You have now calculated dollars per hour worked.

Now, do the same with the amount of money you want to earn. How much would you like to make? How much time would you like to spend working? Divide the former by the latter to obtain your goal number.

We come to the issue that many books on time management try to avoid: your goal number is based on the number of productive hours.

This is a big problem. According to a survey of America's most successful CEOs, an average CEO says that they only produce about 90 productive minutes a day!

Lee Iacocca, the famous auto industry executive, once stated that most CEOs he met in his life didn't have 45 productive minutes in a day.

You may be able to manage a going concern as a CEO working 45 to 90 minutes a day, but it's highly unlikely that you would be able to build a successful business from scratch working the same amount of time.

Success happens when there is a plan and goals are completed quickly.

In the TV Show "The Apprentice," teams compete by completing tasks that would usually take 6 months to a year to complete in a regular environment: tasks such as writing and publishing a book from scratch or developing a marketing campaign from concept to ready-to-go deliverables.

On the show the projects are completed in days, rather than months.

How is this possible, you ask? Very simple! Participants work in an environment with absolutely no distractions.

There are no phones ringing, there are no people being disrespectful of time, and there are no responsibilities like cooking or cleaning. There is a task and there is a deadline. A perfect recipe for how things can get done.

Becoming productive entails scrapping all of your distractions. According to multiple research studies, it takes our brain 20 minutes to get back on a task after an interruption.

Shut off your phone. No calls and no text messages, either. Don't check your emails. Check it only a few times a day.

While it may take you 5 seconds to read an email, your brain will need 20 minutes to get back to when you were on task.

Do people interrupt you a lot? How often do you find yourself in those "Do you have a minute?" conversations that last for over an hour and you feel like you wasted a lot of time, and didn't really accomplish anything?

In order for others to respect you and your time, you need to respect yourself and your time first. The trick in dealing with time vampires who "only need a minute" is very simple: Tell them that you don't have a minute and that you are busy. Follow up by choosing a time when you can help them. Setting a time that is the same every day is the most efficient. If people need a lot of help from you, establish several time periods a day when they can come to you, but make sure it is pre-scheduled.

Have a cut-off time for your meetings. Be available, but determine a stoppage point before starting. Work has a property of spreading itself into whatever time frame it can get.

If someone you are conversing with knows that they have all the time they want, they are more likely to waste it. They might want to talk to you about kids, weather, TV shows and other non-work related stories.

Usually all the small talk nonsense goes away when someone knows that they have your attention for only 15 minutes.

One of the classic problems of entrepreneurs is that there is no imposed work system. When you work for someone else, the employer supplies plan and productivity criteria. The follow-through of the plan is usually supervised by managers. You are held accountable for your efficiency and your success in accomplishing the plan. Imposing structure on individuals causes them to behave in a disciplined manner.

As an entrepreneur you decide what, how and when. Many entrepreneurs simply don't know what to do next when they remove themselves from the structure of a regular job. There is too much freedom. They feel paralyzed and are not sure what to do.

As an entrepreneur, you have to create your own work plan. You must be strict with yourself and set deadlines. Nobody will do this for you. You are on your own. This is the only way.

Conclusion

Thank you again for downloading this book! The advice and suggestions set forth in this book will increase your ability to excel in business. Remember, success is a life-long goal that is organic. When you achieve one level of success, strive to reach the next level as soon as possible.

We must continue to learn new skills in our trade to become proficient and adapt to our changing circumstances. It is important to implement these principles in order to become successful. Most importantly, seek those that are more accomplished than you, because these are the individuals that will help you reach the next level of success in business.